Filibuster

to

Delay

a

Kiss

Random House

New York

Filibuster

to

Delay

a

Kiss

◆

And Other Poems

◆

COURTNEY QUEENEY

RANDOM HOUSE and colophon are registered trademarks of Random House, Inc.

Previous publication information for poems appearing in this work is located on p. 81.

ISBN 978-1-4000-6563-9

LIBRARY OF CONGRESS CATALOGING-IN-PUBLICATION DATA
Queeney, Courtney.
Filibuster to delay a kiss: and other poems / Courtney Queeney.
p.   cm.
ISBN-13: 978-1-4000-6563-9
I. Title.
PS3617.U445F55 2007   811'.6—dc22   2006051084

Printed in the United States of America on acid-free paper

www.atrandom.com

2   4   6   8   9   7   5   3   1

First Edition

FOR MY FATHER

Hope
isn't that young girl anymore,
et cetera, alas.

—Wislawa Szymborska,
"The Century's Decline"

CONTENTS

✦

Filibuster

to

Delay

a

Kiss

Elegy

for

My Mother

◆

Because you are not dead
I will continue
to see you every six or nine months,
each meeting an accident.

This last time I knew from one look
at your body stretched out in the ambulance
that despite the neighbor's panicked phone call,
the crowds clotted on lawns, drawn by red lights
and my arrival—wandering daughter, prodigal
of abandonment—you were nowhere near death.

Of all the nails dropped and forgotten on earth
that this one found a way, pointed end first,
to your head; and that you fell off a ladder
to meet it, skull to rust, is an accident possible only
in a world of your warped god's cause and effect.
The cartoon wound was superficial.
I was glad for your smashed glasses,

which left my face softer, untranslated.
There was no one else to call.

I just want to write, once:
When she died I lost my fear
that I would inherit her shadow,
thread on my mother's madness
sleeve by narrow sleeve. I just want you
buried, silenced under the gravity of dirt.

Go away. Please
don't follow me down the street,
ducking behind trees when I glance back.
Stay in bed when I pull
the severe white sheet over your face,
leave my dreams, don't rise
when I wake, to trail me down
the long hall to the cold eye of the mirror,

Mother
who whines like a cur
at my back door,
begging to be let in.

Notes

for

My Future

Biographer

◆

The dark things I did started young, stayed.

Then I heard a cello and thought,
Oh. That's how you say it.

I could spell and count to a hundred
in several languages, but never learned the words
to help anyone to a church.

There were X number of men;
I couldn't solve for X.

With the chameleon as my model
I greened and glowed outside,
or rippled underwater.
Alone, I was translucent, I was

. . .

barely, but survived myself
those early years,

which prepared me
for the later ones,
when I felt like furniture

and never told the truth.

Confession

♦

Forgive me. There was an oath
I swore to the first man, then betrayed

because I liked the lying down, the loss
of control.
Because there's some male in me.

I was pried overly open,
a gutted fish, and you the stropped knife,
and the exchange depended on violence done
each upon the other. You cut some thing loose.

               She digs under fences.
               Her whimpers have a fang in them.

Now I don't come no matter who calls,
nothing sits right. Fell me,

I'd be perfect timber:
bucked, limbed, quartered,
drawn, delivered.

Burn me. I'd be faithful as ash.

Problems

with

the Eye

+

One semester I stared at diseased eyeballs
for hours, for minimum wage
in the med center basement,

cleaning up scanned photos.
A dull chorus: eye eye eye.
I erased dust specks or hairs

clinging to the camera lens
but couldn't fix anyone's cataracts
or the cyclops child with two eyes

grown together mid-forehead—
he strained the limits of my logic.
I cropped eyes so they loomed like planets,

straightened the orbs, let in light or dark.
I wasn't working any magic,
just sitting in front of a machine

. . .

till I could only feel
where I hurt. When I left my dark
I must have glowed, a quiet ornament,

because though I shadowed the sides of buildings,
training my face toward stone,
men stared me down to silence.

Eye of milk and burst blood vessel,
stagnant pond eye algae-scummed,
scarlet eye bulge,

one eye two eye three eye—
I stared for a thousand hours
until each eye was perfectly captured

in its stage of suffering, and I couldn't see
anything else—at lunch,
on every page, an eye in the negative

glaring white over my book,
or hovering above me, counterfeit moon
as I walked home at midnight.

And when I turned the computer off
the screen's light flickered and dwindled
till the only thing left in its murky square

.   .   .

was me, shrunk and warped—
that mirrored girl a distance, a figure split
from me who held my doubled face

still, our eyes dark, dead-ending
in themselves, her silence
a reminder of how far away I was

from how I had to speak.
But she was just one version of my vision
and when I turned to walk away

she gave me her back.
I had a mouth on me,
and I would sound it out.

The

Anti–Leading Lady

on

Longing

◆

I was in that bar where enough shadow inks
over my face to wear it out.
Then I was in a car, propelled forward
by a series of controlled explosions,
strapped in for safety, aware
that at a certain speed no such thing exists.

When everyone else mooned up at stars, contriving a map,
the stars I saw were ice and dust, secular chips,
so I studied the water stains on my ceiling
till I knew those fissures and ribs
better than the cathedral roof of my own mouth.

I translate love from the hush of a hung-up phone
before a body comes to engage me for an hour.
The sound of new snow falling over old snow
outside my window.

.   .   .

I went on with the wrong men so long
I burnished to a high shine, but always my head
insisted on the front door, the calculated retreat.

Nights, I lower to my floorboards
and negotiate with the wood.

I've never met the male of my kind.

Saint Mother

◆

Mother of masks, she never became
a celebrity, though she fled Milwaukee
to kneel and pray
at Our Lady of Guilt
For Escaping the Tar Paper Polack Shacks

but she did make it married
and to the suburbs,
where she founded
Our Lady of Tricky Physics,
and modeled gravity's unfortunate effects
on beauty: slippage and sag

and subsequent madness.
Our Lady of Annihilation
played God well despite the lack of locusts
or floodwaters at her fingertips. As kids,
we were short and without power
and, therefore, the sinners.

Every night she staged a different passion play,
Our Lady Who Did Not Love Us,
a new crucifixion and granting of guilt.
Each of my breaths helped hammer her on.

. . .

Other churches she founded in our house
were Our Lady of Open Warfare,
Our Lady of the Evil Aside,
and Our Lady of the Beautiful Ruin,
where she'd have me worship yet.

No-Man's-Land

♦

Family was a whitewashed,
milk-toothed word
that couldn't account for the mother

who wept and burnt
the roast if the floor was dirty—
or if it was Tuesday, or there were clouds—

or the father, who always came home
late, whistling,
though he spent his daylight

brokering criminals from prison.
I didn't sit in the backyard
with its trees and screens of shade

to hide from the mother's shrill;
I sat on the front step
pretending to be invisible,

face aimed up the block
to the hope of him, who always put down
his work to sit a minute

.   .   .

before he led through the front door
and I followed, small body
earning a long shadow

as it crossed the threshold,
sinking sun behind us and about
to slip under the edge of my only world,

both of us quiet about what crimes
we would all commit inside
in the name and low note of love.

A
Condensed History
of
Our Childhood:
The Plague Years

◆

When the man with the cart creaked round,
calling for bodies, we hid under our beds
or behind the heavy curtains of our eyelids.
Each of us could have passed
for dead, and been mass buried—
that's how pale we were inside,
how poorly we dumb-showed being kids.
We weren't taught how illness
could jump from parent to child,
but observed that contact often led
to the younger one's death.
Because the mother was an error
and her house had been a waste
she sought to lay waste.
Isolation seemed the safest state
but there was no wall against her.

One by one we blinkered our eyes
and sighed out every candle.
We pinched our tongues
and locked our meager mouths.
We agreed to forget to the same degree,
which meant forever,
because erasure
was our only anesthetic.
Our history was rewritten,
leaving out the dark ages.
We were, it read,
beginning to end.

Unmedicated

◆

I.

I am staid or sad.

In the morning I rise dress and shine
or am trussed, adrift, shorn.

I have a small measure of calm
or can't muster myself.
Alone or lonely, driven or riven,
toothless or ruthless.

The sidewalk's a flock of cracks,
the street rife with omens: ravens
lined like sentries on a drooping black bough,
gravel drive dead-ending at a razed garage.

II.

At one party I lean against a wall.
There's a well inside
I'm working on.

. . .

When the male
who's been trying to breathe me under him
who'd like me breathless and edible

stalks over, attractive as a trap,

I learn the wall.
I don't let him part me.

When he leaves I index my emotions:
Rather, Blather,
Constant Blue About the Lips.

III.

The other man's my opposite.

He bedded me while I was unlevel,
I was raised devil to the second power.

He nursed my hurt
but I can't send away
my own set weight. I've tried.

Once I had a knack.
Now I'm knuckled under.

The

Trouble

with

Openings

◆

is they unclose you, your body
become an invitation to pillage.
You let a man burgle your organs
then feed him before he flees
out the window, down the fire escape.
You say, *Come back anytime, I'll be in.*
I've been deflead, my shots are up to date.
Then he's gone and you're left
with only all your wide-open empties
which spread, and burrow through your walls,
and admit so much.

Bone-Break Fever

◆

I. Santo Domingo: Dengue Fever

The women taking my temperature shake.
My head will not hold them steady.

The doctor totters moving the IV
from one swollen elbow hinge
to puncture my wax hand.

Veins break and bloom in my dumb claw.
I reduce to a spine, a wing of hips
on white sheets, a flattening.

In sun the orchids shiver.
At night they glow,
a clot of calm eyes.

They're tokens of the outside
world, which still moves
past the window curtain
and the man who sent them,
his name dissolved under my tongue.

. . .

Every four hours I'm infused with fluids
inserted in stages. I drought.
The nurse brings steaming liver,
fatty ham, sausages sweating oil
into the air. The orchids bloat,
learning to be carnivores.

II. Bone-Break Fever: Precautionary Measures

The first time you catch it
you shake so hard you slam
the metal bedrail staccato against the wall.
You'll cool but your blood's been breached.

The second time
your bones are tricked into feeling fractured,
though you're only touched on the quarter-hour,
and then gently. You don't own enough hands
to reach the deep itch. The fever earns its name.

The third time your veins collapse, you bleed
into the sack of your skin, out your eye sockets.
There is no fourth time.

To prevent infection
hang a net around your bed.

III. Syracuse: Love as Disease

I don't want this gift of a single orchid—
maroon, small-petaled blooms laddered up a woody stem.

The ones on trees aren't parasites;
their roots suck fuel from the air.
My orchid's rootless, and temporary.
It wasn't meant to live, just ornament.

My cat knocks the vase over,
then ignores the righted orchid.
She understands disdain.

Its stem is skinny as my spinster hands.
It's a scarlet ideogram printed against the harem
stage-set of my curtains, matte against satin.

Some orchids witch as an insect, or an insect's enemy,
or an insect's mate. Some stink like rotting meat
to pollinate. I don't want

want, or an orchid—from the Greek for *testicle*—
or the man, trying to insinuate his body into my room
through this surrogate flowering.
He says things like *Look at the moon*

.   .   .

that don't melt me. The moon looks like
the white pills in my medicine cabinet
but less calm.

With no natural enemies save weather and disease
orchids can, in a perfect environment, live forever.

This orchid is a red ribbon
wound round my neck,
keeping my head on, cutting me
dead from the neck down.

Vestigial

◆

Because she's stuck with herself
she scalpels out mother, father, ghosts.

Some boys, some men. She spits out
Sorry and *Maybe* and *After you*

and the mean things never let fly from her mouth
that buzzed around that wet cavern like wasps

till she couldn't think linear. With three
well-placed incisions, she slips out of her hide.

She excises the seductive tongue,
fallopian tubes in an upside-down Y

like an unsnapped wishbone,
then detaches pelvis from hip socket,

wrought to bear, to bear
down. All soft tissue. All soft.

Because erasure is impossible she strips
white bundles of nerves, those liars

· · ·

who jump to attention under any
outlawed hand. The meat of her thigh.

She bargains with her heart, that blood organ
which has backed her into too many corners,

but she can't override its pulse or fancy.
She saves her marionette tendons,

spares the clean ligament strings.
She hoards bile, incisors, clicking spine.

Bled safe, she is a set of loosely linked
hard parts, an audience evolved

for her four white walls.

Reckoning

◆

I received the bill for my beautiful lunatic
mother. Now that she's sagged
and grayed, she costs more, she and her brother,

my uncle who sits silent in forests for hours,
imitating the trees in order to kill animals
in the old way, with a bow and arrow, like a real man,
and only then makes it home

to my cousin, his daughter who hasn't swallowed in years
because she's always just about to choke to death

and her brother who keeps inventing
insistent cancers in his brain and lungs,
all hidden from the severe eye of the X-ray.

But my silent dragged-down aunt doesn't cost much—
she doesn't challenge the wallpaper,
she folds into corners and mimics the dining room chairs.

My grandmother with her saints
and hierarchy of trespass
racked up surcharge after surcharge, her

and her goddamned bakery cinnamon bread
we'd eat after church

and for which I had to say *thank you*
and each *thank you* bored another small hole
in my already black-bit heart,

and Christ dying for my sins,
over and over,

so even with my undersized lungs offered up
alongside my unbalanced eyes, my cold shoulder,
my left hand, my hair shorn, my X
on the dotted line—taxed,
spent and wanting—
I still owe.

Conviction

◆

When I was young it was easy to walk out
while my parents slept upstairs, to stalk
the winding ravine road, where families of raccoons

rustled under the droning streetlights
in loose lines of rounded bodies
to ransack the neighbors' neatly packaged trash.

This was the suburbs, I couldn't feel God anywhere,
I could see my mother's eyes abandoned like the hallway
of a burning building: vacant, loaded with smoke.

She talked sin in a voice increasingly loud
and aimed at me—first daughter, first danger—
but according to the rules laid out,

as I understood them, if I murdered my mother,
but confessed and did penance, and truly regretted,
I could still go to heaven, where I knew

she'd never be. This seemed a technicality, a loophole
too close to a noose, but I kept it on hold, nights
when I wandered, dared Him to shove me down the ravine,

. . .

break me to prove He was there, witness to my irreverence,
but He never hurt me the way I'd learned to hurt.
Since I couldn't walk out of my skin or skull

and into a more acceptable version of girl,
I prayed to mirrors so I wouldn't disappear,
I pinched my forearm in algebra. I always was,

somehow, there: waiting
for the blessing of any touch, girl
who would have killed for a single conviction.

Upper-Crust
Adolescence

♦

For the first boy, I was one in a series of drugs.
I dulled his whiskey-warmth to sleep

and a month later, he checked into a clinic
in the coldest north of our country.

The second was an aspiring scientist
who wanted me well-lit and pinned

to a bed, or flattened between glass
and slid under a microscope's precise eye.

Although I knew scrutiny
was not sex, because I was unschooled

save in silence and the pliant *Yes*
the cataloguing of parts continued.

The girls in my town didn't have a dark river
or a wooden bridge to moon around,

· · ·

just a crumbling bluff, dun colored,
and a steady, slow erosion

that never hurt the real estate market.
Parents liked their homes precarious

and large over a long fall into water.
There was always some boy

to kiss under the buzzing streetlight
filling my head with static, closest state to a swoon

I'd allow, though I wanted them to swallow me whole
or spirit me away from the house

where my mother was the epicenter
of every earthquake,

and the approaching apocalypse
would be homegrown, and expensive.

Love Song
for
the Boy
Who Got Away

•

I got the belt unbuckled, chest unveiled,
partial panic at the thought of him naked
and then he fled, left me without the numb,
eye-shut, seasick in the swells and exhales,
loving the ocean; without that after-sag,
blood hum and flesh plush, lazy slick of thighs,
before I remember I have eyes
and body parts go shy again and snag
and I surrender my temporary grace.
My advances weren't reimbursed.
I never got a morning to wake first,
study his single, unguarded face.
He was gone for maybe five minutes, then
he had always been gone.

Freak:

A

One-Woman

Show

◆

When I spackle on a public skin
over a quarter decade's pointillist mess

these eyes blue in their black sockets,
two targets. Hit me. Scarlet strumpet

mouth won't rub off, I'm good
with what God gave, I turn my own corners

up with a pencil. Done, this face is so white
I blend into his bare walls

then glow holy in the bar outside town
where I'm an itinerant star—

mirage of dust and ice, already dead
when he picks me up, and drives me cold

• • •

to a cracked booth, its sticky duct-taped rift
spewing stuffing. We maneuver

a chipped table between us,
my sleeves dragging in wet rings,

then he lets me talk twenty minutes
before he leans in close enough

to let me know the music's too loud,
baby, what'd I say? eyes above my head

to the TV where men in garish spandex
take turns running at each other like bulls.

I bring my tears to a bathroom stall
so I won't scare away the kid

in him, enough breath left
to fog the mirror and write another one

of my thousand evaporating
fan letters he'll never read

over scratched glass.
Then I wipe what I've admitted

· · ·

off with my palm—
I don't need an audience

to sleep at night—and juke out
to the cover band wailing,

and sweep on my coat in the parking lot,
cracking black ice beneath my feet.

I concentrate on the small weather
my mouth breathes in his car too old

to warm, leaving a lace of frost
across the windshield for him

to stare through for another one of his winters,
and I can see his mouth moving, man,

but nothing's coming through.

Filibuster

to

Delay

a

Kiss

⁺

I invoked the dictionary's authority—*Incidental* to *Incompatible,*
Juvenile Hormone to *Kangaroo, Keeper* to *Ketchup,*
Plain People to *Planned Parenthood, Yokel* to *Yuck*—
then segued into ingredients from a cereal box side panel,
the noble gases: helium, neon. When I forgot my own chemistry,
I rattled off one page of the phone book, Smith to Smith,
then argued against drilling for oil in the Arctic,
then shut my eyes to describe the windshield's panopticon from
     memory,
then opened them and fugued lyrically on ocean reeds—
all so he'd lose interest, wander off—I recited Woolf's last letter,
floundered through Hamlet's *To be or not to be,* mustered
synonyms for *alone, insulated, aloof,* because at any break
I knew there'd be the hand over my mouth.
There'd be his mouth.

Invitation

♦

for Sarah C. Harwell

The invitation that never came claimed, *Come, this should be fun,*
and being a sucker for events where I'm unwanted
I shrugged on my prettiest face and the shirt I wear

to be tastefully naked in public, I cultivated each eyelash.
By the time Sidekick honked outside I'd talked down
to my mirror for hours, and was ready to hole up at home,

but Sidekick insisted we circle the party in her car,
practicing the smoldering looks we'd bless the men with,
imagining the way each one would sit in shadow,

though some of them we bargained back down to boys
renamed Flimsy, Slipknot, Inflation. Eroded egos
shored up by the wailing radio, which advertised our options

as either: a) happily ever after, or b) a lifetime of wretchedness,
we entered the usual awkward: the host was large with light,
he had a love, everyone else was half of a pair.

. . .

Sidekick and I gnawed at stale bread crusts like the prisoners we
    were.
We took down a book and read some dead men aloud
to stave off despair, which worked for ten or eleven minutes.

Then I exiled myself to the porch to phone people
scattered across other hours, my real friends, and confess
Some of us here will be utter failures and *I am not immune,*

but when I couldn't reach anyone in my same state
of intoxication, I tottered home on my stilts
along the park where girls wearing pheromones like mine

are violated or disappeared,
and called my sleeping father, and spoke into his answering
    machine
as fast as I forgot what I needed to say,

messages he would hear
a year from now, a thousand miles away, yesterday.

The

Anti-Leading Lady

Dissociates

+

Some days I approximate a vacant lot.
Instead of fire I have a face—a solid
slow-flowing, a target's white and heart
and near unhittable. There is no heat
or wavelength of radiance to reach me
in my assemblage of bones, this scaffold
that props me upright and adult. I leave
my name at home when I go out in crowds,
swallowing my blank, untutored tongue.
Some lies light, others shadow. My right hand shuns
the left, vocal cords divorce the lungs,
nerve endings split from the spine. From no one
nothing can be taken. I swear,
there's someone home, but I don't own her.

Separation

Anxiety

◆

Border: *a margin, rim, or edge.*
Mother as cliff I'll dive off.
Mother I shove into the closet,
tuck under the rug.

Border: *a frontier area separating*
political or geographical boundaries.
Mother as Uzbekistan, Rwanda,
an enemy engagement. Mother as Other.

And Line: *The locus of a point having one degree of freedom.*
One degree can be enough to breathe, thrive, leave.

Line, as if drawn in the sand:
        Come over come over I dare you.
Or worse:
        You are already on my side.

Descended from Thread,
the disease vows
You are tied to me.
I will never let you go.

All My Mothers

◆

One of my mothers never held me,
another soldered her hands around my neck.

My mother who quilts links fabric scraps
into large, patterned expanses
she hangs to warm the walls

though she'd leave her needles
to rip phones out of walls, fling clean laundry
from a second-story window to stipple the lawn,
then boil spaghetti and ask each child
how its day was.

My indecisive mother liked to make me walk miles in snow
to another house for shelter, then call the cops to pick me up—
one way to celebrate my birthday.
My happy mother is caught in yellowing photographs
and died when I was born

but a restless one still prowls the static on my phone.
She's the ghost of my voice.

My gold mother is an idol of an extinct religion;
I never rubbed her stomach for luck.

My green mother hated that we looked alike, and I was always
    younger.
My red mother flung her tongue around and set my bed on fire.

My mother with chameleon hair
keeps moving the numerals fixed to the front of her new house
then inviting me over to locate her locked door.

My ringmaster mother can't keep a dog or cat alive more than
    three months,
though civilizations of thriving flies circle her kitchen's collapsing
    fruit
and her bread blooms mold in abstract patterns.

Based on this, you could say she does support life
but only in select forms.

My Alzheimer's disease mother insists, *You had a happy childhood*
and can't remember any waning in the children.

My conspiracy-theory mother can prove
my father brainwashed and bribed.
Before she was paranoid she was Miss Midwest.

One of my mothers I haven't spoken to in seven years.
One of my mothers is mute, and we have never spoken.

.   .   .

One of my mothers suffers from bad gums and blood
that shudders too quickly through her veins.
She'll end up in a hospital with some old-age ailment,
and maybe then I'll be able to touch her hand
without grinding her finger bones till she begs, *Mercy.*

She stands over me while I sleep
swelling to fill the room.
She breathes with me, she won't leave
till I can utter nothing
save her name.

The
Anti-Leading Lady's
Nightmare

◆

It was October. I was between men.

I loved autumn. Sudden cold fronts,
and when I walked, crunching leaves under my feet,
I sounded like smashing glass.

Then the two men were flanking me.
They were not supposed to meet like this—
on the street, unexplained. We walked
into the setting sun. I was the wedge between them.

No hard feelings, I said. I didn't steal anyone's anything.

It's hard to walk down a sidewalk between two men,
with all the friction of hips and swinging arms,
and the sunset rendered beautifully
through its filter of pollution.

I was just hungry, I said. Deal with it. You're men.

·   ·   ·

We entered a long hall. They held me up;
my legs wouldn't lock or step
as we passed the rows of identical cages
to the room of the serious electricity.

How did we get here? I asked. Is this a metaphor?

One of them put a finger to his lips.
At midnight, for a moment, the lights dimmed.

Love Song

of

the Insomniac

and

the Narcoleptic

+

Always she ends up
an audience to his breaths.
She does love him purely, just partly—

there are so many other kneecaps,
shoulders, lower lips, chins.
He's meat, face-planted in a pillow.

She curls shut as a cocktail shrimp
on his flimsy couch, sorting
through reasons to unhook her

from him, exaggerating when it helps,
urged on by the blue wash
of the mute TV

.   .   .

while he heats a halo all ways
round his long body.
When she can't rally a crowd

of reasons to leave
she thumbs through the masses inside,
hunting down an appropriate persona

to replace the traitor
who is ready to swear
I never wanted this to end

when it ends, because she
has always been a liar. His eyes
rove and jerk under their thin-veined lids.

Nothing happens,
except the clock
creeps on toward the first dun

wash of dawn and the next train
with its desperate wail and trundle.
He sets in sleep. She kindles

to her same dim flame.

The
Anti-Leading Lady's
Libido

◆

I wish I had her on a leash, taught
to fetch, sit, heel.
Instead she abandons me

the whole heavy month of July,
the air swollen with water, rain
like tongues licking my skins,

slicking me
ready. She's rutting
around in the bushes,

doesn't come when I call out
in the dark, but lopes off
across the empty lot

about to be cleared of brush and built over.
On the stoop I listen for her footfalls.
Without her I'm packed sand—

.   .   .

weighty, dewinged. I sag and listen
for the train every two A.M.,
its long nasal wail

an alarm bell sounding my emergency,
tolling against this body stuck
yet shaken.

Refrain

◆

The assorted men in white coats diagnosed me as lack of sleep
but I've never slept eight hours nightly, and this unsettling

at the edges of my vision, the flashing lights, was new.
Ghost insects. Waver shakes. Lightning in the negative.

Objects stood still when I looked at them straight.
Wandering around the municipal city with its severe white
    noons

and packs of roving pigeons and spoked rotaries
so I'd have to cross three streets just to make a right angle,

I kept hearing the men at the car wash mumble, *Courtney
Courtney*, and then the plaid and pearled couples

carrying their tiny manicured dogs were slipping it in
their chat, *Courtney*, but meant for me to hear

and I heard and I thought *Even my breakdowns
will be keyed to this name, my ego's only note.*

· · ·

And then I couldn't stand my gray self thrown back in plate
    glass,
or talk to cashiers with their *Hi* or *How you doing* while my items
    scanned

with that red laser I'd heard could strike you blind.
    I couldn't consume.
I could lay round his apartment and consider the rain

and later I could crouch on the floor and attend to his sleep,
air conditioner rattling like a hive. The flaw with trying to reason

myself free was my brain, both the fault
and the only hold I had. There was calm

to swallow in milligrams, but still I'd lock myself
in the antiseptic bathroom whose white tiles multiplied

to try to ration my breath back down to human
so I could dial everyone I knew on the West Coast, where people

were still awake, and if anyone answered the phone
I'd ask, thick-tongued but quick as I knew how,

Don't you know who this is?

Triage

◆

At the hospital I grovel for oxygen,
ready to trade any sham dignity still clinging
for a shot or pill to tamp

the panic down, head
between my knees.
I sit and heave till my face numbs

like a cut of beef on ice
and black winged bodies
crow through the hallway, migrating nowhere.

The unfortunate and accidental are treated first.
I find this fair. I surrender my shoelaces
to the police escort who wants to know

what the hell I'm doing here,
blood at the back of my throat, taped gauze
pulling the fine hairs on my forearm.

He's procedure
for the desperate and stupid—
the drunk boy with the skinned torso and face

•   •   •

who slurs into a phone, *Fuck you,* argues with the wall,
I'm not drunk, feet bare on the speckled tile,
and our homeless ghost who slit one wrist

shallowly, for the free breakfast.
He's propped on his side like an obscene centerfold.
In the litany of wounds and wrongs, mine is

an ignorance of how to alchemy a new me
from this waste and shame.
I haven't bled my inner plague out or burned pure.

I am no magic trick. When I shut my eyes
they disappear,
I don't.

Fame:

My Version

◆

Somehow in the seeking
I confused *fame* with *frame*:
I pressed my face to picture windows
of houses I couldn't afford to live in,
I folded myself into the dumbwaiters
of old ornate hotels.
None of this was picked up by the press.
I spent my mornings constructing
model houses from toothpicks and glue.
A lonely labor, though some
who had gone before me
had achieved immortality
through a similar attention to form.
While some men fingerprinted me
no charges were ever filed,
my grim profile never graced a post office wall.
The only public estimates had me
as rumor, and my public had shrunk
to five or six individuals
since I'd ceased to speak with the voice
I was born to. In the sole home movie

that survived my childhood
I appear in one exposure—
there I am, blink, I'm gone.
A million hands clapping
while I flamed out still nameless.

Inheritance

◆

When I bury my body
in my twilight bed, muzzled,
curled kneecap to chin, my spine
cheap beads on a strained string,
you're the stingy bellows for my lungs,
Mother—you're the hand held
over my mouth.

Or when I am acting my own traitor again,
seeking asylum in the anonymous skin
of a man, you're unstitching the zipper,
steel-toothed as I remember you.
This cage is your bones
with my skin stretched over.
You linger in every bald mirror.

Or when I walk down a street
inches away from leaning into its blur
of speeding cars—orphan of velocity,
up for adoption to any element more fluid
than this one stuck shape, its corrupt blood—
you're itching to give me that littlest nudge.
You call this love.

Rhymes With

◆

Mother who threw my clothes on the front lawn: a hint.
Mother who crashed pots against pans, a cliché in a kitchen.

Mother as the burglar rifling through my genetic code,
who won't obey the logic that argues her away, every twilight,
   every man.

Mother as the riot in me, Mother as my unappeasable mob.
Mother as *the ailment that affects normal, healthy functioning.*

She mothered the disorder in me,
this difficulty getting out of bed

and dressing like a real human adult,
trying not to be her daughter:

looks like laughter,
rhymes with slaughter.

The
Anti–Leading Lady's
Self-Defense

◆

Once upon a time I fell in love—
an accident with injuries.

I thought I'd die without him,
on some sort of stage-set, propped
and spotlit, soap operatic.
But all the evidence was against us:
few animals mate for life in the wild,
girls on the radio sound sassier but not happy,
I'm attached to my own last name.

Maybe I should have read more fairy tales as a child;
I read a lot of Vonnegut.

Bedroom is an anagram for *boredom.*
I heard this on the radio. *Passion* and *suffering*
share the same root, and this can't be a coincidence.

Love is fire, love is heat. Females leak,
and people are plants.

Seeing is touching.
Staying alive is a contest.

Can someone unloved early and thoroughly
love back? All those studies about infants untouched
by their mothers. The someone is the speaker.

At first our hands have no urgency.
The other parts, once we've begun the fumblings,
friction into their own momentum
and save us.

The truth is, underneath
I have no negotiating power,
being born blue-early and a year too soon,
set in a hot box, skinny limbs warmed by a lamp.
Kept apart and unheld, electricity
was my mother-love, and now,
bodies falter.

Time is a devourer, healer, evaluator.
Time is a pursuer, reaper, thief.

My welcome mat reads *I never met a man
I couldn't leave.*
Like my other public declarations
it's mostly bluff and exoskeleton,
but no one comes and knocks at night.

. . .

When love ends, we break up.
We crack up in the loony bin.
The parlance is not so disparate;
the severings are similar.

It's always three A.M. and love,
the only language I have for you
is paradox and loss, and mean—
as in small, and stingy.

The word *happy* is kin to luck and chance.

Today it rained and even the garbage
in the courtyard looked scrubbed,
and the neighbor's windowsill row of sunflowers
stretched their necks to the sun, dripping,
and I could have loved anyone at all, forever,
for a half-hour.

My tombstone to read:
Restless, restless, restless.

Tourist

♦

I wandered round the husk
of the oldest cathedral in this hemisphere
with its bodied, bloody suffering.
My mother was everywhere in me. I couldn't rout her.

The saints statued around Santo Domingo
had rain-eroded faces, the frescoed women
painted pink and white as wedding cake.
She wouldn't be shaken,

she had the same flat eyes as the plastic Mary
at a highway shrine, caged against vandals.
Around her base, a heap of plastic water bottles
cast a fluid shadow skirt,

though this Mary was gone from the waist down.
I'd exiled myself to another mother tongue
because I hoped distance would translate into asylum,
and icon or parable refract her

into something simple enough to understand.
But she'd lodged in me, body and blood,
as if I let her dissolve in my mouth
every morning, my only religion, saved by her,

. . .

but I wasn't. At night,
under the smoky lights of a club,
I salted to a high shine, I led temptation home
and delivered myself to any other evil.

Eloping Alone

✦

Dear Man:

I'm leaving you my overbloomed ghetto of a garden and my
    spinster cat. Her hysteria's been scalpeled out and sutured
    over. I'm taking my ring finger with me, my whitest sheets.

I realize in an earlier century I would already be installed in the
    attic of a luckier sibling with a pair of knitting needles and an
    obligation to the bloodiest slaughters, canning vegetables by
    candlelight while the others bed down with hot flannel-
    wrapped bricks at their feet. I understand in another country
    I could be killed for flaunting my delicate wrists and ankles.

But I'm sick of washing the dishes while you press against me
    from behind, like every unfulfilled naughty housewife fantasy
    I never had. I'm too full of tremors, and you don't have enough
    years in you.

I hope you find the girl you deserve, the one with no fruit flies,
    who'll swell some kids into the world bearing the average of
    your two ordinary faces. She'll quiet at night, and wake
    according to the clock.

· · ·

These aren't shivers, they're a shaking off. It's a really neat trick I turn, it's one of my dozen disappearing acts.

Your,

X.

Nocturnal

Housekeeping

◆

I till the baseboard dust but nothing live rises under my hands.
My imaginary husband says, *Wash my shirts and socks, would you?*

I have no clean underwear. The children we never bore
trail crumbs on the floor for me to follow, threshold to threshold.

Always around a corner, or in a closet, they press their sticky
    hands to walls
like convicts trying to tally and order their countdown hours.

Under the burned-out bulb this stove will never scrub clean
but I scour onward, chemicals furrowed into the rivers of my
    fingerbeds,

while my made-up man crowds behind to witness
this eleventh hour of failure, sighing into the back of my neck.

My fridge is weeks lukewarm but I wipe it clean then close it
on its own stale air. The curtains snap, sopped with rain;

the windows will be white with dust again by morning.
    Untouched,
the front door slams shut. My dead bolt slides home.

Astigmatism

◆

My cornea's warp shivers you, love, staggers
the straight line of your spine. Lensless,
you're blur, a body quivering in place,
a gesture stopped with film of the wrong speed,

then run through an X-ray machine.
I'd like to see your silhouette clear
on my own, flip you upside down in each eye,
carry you on the million tiny nerves that shuttle

light to my brain. It's less than a second, but first
you exist as electricity pulsing, and my imperfect parts
haven't yet failed to bring you into focus:
cornea like a watch crystal,

finely muscled iris, lens of accommodation.
The pupil, constantly learning light and shadow
from scratch. In each eye, the optic disc,
my built-in blind spot.

Recurring Dream

◆

In the one dream where I'm actually kind,
my mother knocks on my door
and I admit her. Actually,

I'm out of my chair before her hand
raps the wood, I can feel her coming
with that weird dream clairvoyance—

and I'm asking already
as I swing the door wide
enough to let in the world,

Why didn't you come sooner?
asking the familiar, silent black.
In the dream I don't have

there are people in a room, sitting
quiet, if not happy. No one
gets up and leaves.
No one has ever been left.

Ghazal

of

the Ungotten

◆

Wine unscrews my locks, blinkers my logic, lops off my rudder.
Midnight makes you, streetlight scalene across your face, less of
an error.

All your rooms are bare wood, spare and scared of their own spiders.
I'd allow you to serve the chaos where I live. I'd even pay you a
quarter.

If you're an idol, eye paint rubbed away by pilgrim thumbs for luck,
if you're an ancient scroll, a holy splinter, stained glass, then why
do you waver?

Nothing moves me the rare moments I'm stone, nothing courses.
Electricity evolved from the Greek *electrōn*, an old word for
amber.

Recently I've had to concentrate on continuing the common
inhale and exhale.
I'm a stuttering schoolgirl failing a test, an understudied young
stammer.

. . .

Our particular dramatic production has too many actors vying
    for its two leads.
We're like *Titus*: Lavinia's hands and tongue are cut out, and it's
    humor.

I will fly around the world on an airplane until I arrive at calm.
I will spend my days suspended in air, manufacturing a closure.

Days are manic scarlet, tart, silk, capable carnivore with rows of
    teeth.
Nights are drear, scullery, grunge, darned, altogether underworn
    by another.

My desire is a pale girl with a great imagination. She thinks
    Paradise is boring.
You say, *Lock her up in your darkest closet, I'll call you later.*

I survived a long time off the smell of your neck, the fold of your
    cuff.
I died a long time from the radio at midnight, your tendency to
    wander.

I courted the boast in you, the marrow, the wonder of ten new
    knuckles.
Man, I meant some of it tender. Once in a while you were.

First Failed Career

◆

I wanted to record my breathing in sleep
and send it to some Third World country
where it would soothe all the mewling orphans

in their identical orphan cribs
and they'd be able to live happily
in consummated monogamous marriages

feeling only as stifled and restless
as the rest of their country's indigenous peoples,
and not all warped and lonely

because they never had a mother heart beat—
because I've had that trouble, finding a heartbeat—

but I was afraid the tape would be pirated
and sold as an expensive sleep machine setting
wasted on people who already own what they need:

Ocean Waves, Whale Song,
Woman Sleeping Through Hurricane Season.

The

Current

Courtney Ann Queeney

◆

As a girl she thought her middle name was *And,* and ran with it:
a common word to link first to last. She was corrected early on.

Courtney Queeney is the subject and object
of the prison sentence, the stage, the obituary.
She parades whichever face
will get her some plunder, a title, or out the door.

Courtney Queeney is an anatomy of melancholy
written in egg white and cipher. On the page she yellows
but hold her up to a lightbulb and she'll break.

With bread stuck in her throat, she's a contraction with no air,
the absence in attendance. You can pass a hand through her.

Courtney Queeney can only conceive of love as a leaving,
in the negative, and not. Her cat is teaching her
the advantages of nocturnal clawing.

. . .

Courtney Queeney is the punch line to a dumb joke
her lawyer father made
though she is neither regal nor litigious.

Eventually she'll donate her skewed eyes to science;
meanwhile, *Courtney Queeney* almost rhymes with *ennui*

and wonders why so many birds nest in her walls.
She lies awake at night and attends their muffled flutters.

Confessed, confirmed, and dechurched,
some days her head floats
to the ceiling, a released balloon,

and even when she hallucinates it's her own name
she hears, Courtney Courtney Courtney—

she doesn't think her arms deserve
to be pretty, they're such narcissists, mirroring
whatever body is nearest. She wants to start and end here.

My
Future
as the
Farmer's Wife

•

I'd be the scarecrow with crows perched up and down
my hard straw arms, he'd be greasy-handed, tinkering
with the tractor while our crops crisped under steady sun,
our homestead omened around the county
by the blinking *Controlled Burning Ahead* sign, the kind
you see at the sides of highways, no flames in sight.
We'd get married for the baby we'd lose,
but later make more kids to run
smear-mouthed in front of the thresher,
step on rusty nails, set the barn on fire.
The cats, bundles of twigs,
would cringe round my ankles
while I chew cud like the rest of the heifers,
list in my slippers and slot dishes
on the drying rack and wish the crows
would get their own corn. I'm already tired
talking about the weather—when will it frost,
when will it snow, where's the rain?

I wasn't made to sit and watch things grow.
Every day he'll bring in earth—
bootsoles stepping out of neat mud grids,
grit rubbed from his forearms
onto the kitchen towels, edging his nails.
All the animals here owned
in the name of the husband.
At five o'clock, we'll clamor to be fed.

Back

t o

the Body

✦

If I'm arch, you're thrust. If I'm pocket,
you're muscle, kneecap, and skid. If I sit,
you're canvas, man, two eyes gone darker in the dark.
If I'm dark, you're insistent fingers.

I'm hinge to your lock and push, bare-toed,
uneasy in my skin and then the skin
forgotten. You're the bruise on my back
in half-circles of hunger, tongue, and hush.

If you're a spread of chest, I lay me down,
audience and song. If you're altar
I kneel before you. Here I am,
animal.

The Light

◆

In my thirteenth year I dragged.
At the doctor's I drank the glass of chalk
like a good girl,

and when the allotted hour was up
he fed my body
into the prehistoric black machine,

big as a room. The barium I swallowed
illuminated a screen, my body
abnormal and incandescent,

so he slid me back out of its belly
and carved my neck into sections
with black ink, marks he measured

limit to limit, to map my thyroid swollen.
There was a slowly dying star
expanding inside my throat. It choked

me when I tried to eat. For weeks
I couldn't breathe, as the dosage
was raised and lowered, chasing my blood's

•   •   •

imbalance. At dinner I'd cry
above my untouched plate, struggle
to set my face; at dawn, I'd cackle in my lit room,

pacing its cage, wondering
when I would get my body back.
Eventually I'd lie down, possessed,

restless with an alien energy,
and wait for the glow
I knew my body would give off, myself

the light at the end of the tunnel.

ACKNOWLEDGMENTS

✦

"Confession," "Elegy for My Mother," and "Nocturnal Housekeeping" appeared in *American Poetry Review.* "Back to the Body," "No-Man's-Land," and "The Trouble with Openings" appeared in *Lyric.* "Notes for My Future Biographer" appeared in *MARGIE.* "The Anti-Leading Lady Dissociates," and "Eloping Alone" appeared in *McSweeney's.* "Vestigial" appeared in *Salmagundi.* "Notes for My Future Biographer," "Problems with the Eye," "Confession," "The Anti-Leading Lady on Longing," "Reckoning," "Filibuster to Delay a Kiss," "Invitation," "All My Mothers," "Inheritance," "Eloping Alone," "Astigmatism," "Recurring Dream," "Ghazal of the Ungotten," "First Failed Career," "The Current Courtney Ann Queeney," "My Future as the Farmer's Wife," and "The Light" appeared in *Three New Poets,* Sheep Meadow Press, March 2006.

Grateful acknowledgment to Daniel Menaker for editorial guidance, and to everyone at Random House who helped usher this book into the world; I owe a huge debt to the Syracuse University Writing Program for funding and support when I was the hungriest, and to my teachers Michael Burkard, Brooks Haxton, Chris Kennedy, George Saunders, and Bruce Smith for their generous attention to my work; and pitifully inadequate thanks to Mary Karr, to whom I owe everything. For company during the crucial years, thanks to Sarah C. Harwell, Micha Boyett Hohorst, Farah Marklevits, Gerry Lambert, and Immy Wallenfells. These poems could not have been written without Josh and the enormous yes; for solidarity through the dark ages, love to Bob, Maggie, Alex, and my father.

COURTNEY QUEENEY was born in Chicago in 1978. She is a graduate of the Creative Writing Program at Syracuse University. Her poetry has appeared in *American Poetry Review, McSweeney's,* and elsewhere. She lives in New York City.

◆

Jenson is one of the earliest print typefaces. After hearing of the invention of printing in 1458, Charles VII of France sent coin engraver Nicolas Jenson to study this new art. Not long after, Jenson started a new career in Venice in letter-founding and printing. In 1471, Jenson was the first to present the form and proportion of this roman font that bears his name.

More than five centuries later, Robert Slimbach, developing fonts for the Adobe Originals program, created Adobe Jenson based on Nicolas Jenson's Venetian Renaissance typeface. It is a dignified font with graceful and balanced strokes.